The Morning Cup.
A 21-Day Devotional For the 21st Century Believer

By: Marissa Farrow, M.Div.

Library of Congress Cataloging-in-Publication Data

ISBN: 9798329738100

Published by Marissa Farrow LLC.

For permission requests, contact the publisher at
Info@MarissaFarrow.com

Printed in UNITED STATES

First Edition

Dedication

This book is dedicated to you Sham, Sham, may you forever know what your life has taught me. That is the power of prayer. You drew me closer to God than I ever knew I could be. Daily I needed direction, to ensure I didn't drop the gift of you and, it has made me the better. "luhhh youuuuu.." Forever and always.

-Your "God"mom

Table of Contents

INTRODUCTION:

THE POWER OF PRAYER

For as long as I can remember, prayer has been a part of my life. Not only because my dad has been pastoring for more than twice my life span, but my entire family has seemingly been raised to understand the priority, pilgrimage, and power of prayer. Prayer wasn't optional in my family. To be clear, it wasn't forced down our throats or impressed upon us as "mandatory to meet the master one day," either. It was more like, just present. It was always around us. Always happening. It was a part of every significant moment we faced as a family. So, prayer became a place of peace even before my brain could fully comprehend the true mechanism of this type of intimacy and access to the God of the entire universe! With prayer setting the pace for everything we did as a household and within my family at large, it easily became the priority because, at that age, it seemed like making prayer the priority would allow you to enter any moment in peace. You must think about the mind of a 7, 8, and 9-year-old girl who constantly sees her family using prayer as what I can only describe as a weapon of peace and power. That if you want to accomplish anything, you must first wave this wand of prayer, because prayer will essentially prepare the way for whatever you are seeking to do. If it's needing strength to go into a funeral service or wisdom and protection to run around the theme park all day long with your friends. Returning to school each year, whatever we did, we carried this weapon of prayer before us. "So, Marissa, what do you mean? Like, were you literally on your knees at five, six, and seven years old? Is that why I can't think of the words to pray like you?" You'd be surprised at how many people ask me that all around the world. "How do you find the words to pray for things like that?" I would consider myself very blessed.

When I was a little girl, my favorite thing in the world was to hang out with my dad, who was a very active full-time pastor, carpenter, graphic design artist, and freelance painter. It's safe to say I got it, honest. So, you're liable to see me with a mic, camera, or computer. Preaching, producing, or designing. He was a ball of fun, I'd get everything I wanted, and my mom was off being a superhero in Washington, DC. at the time, I didn't know that God would order my steps this way because my mother was breaking barriers as a woman in corporate government finance, while my dad was this awesome pastor and hustler, if you asked me. He was never not working. So, in my travels with my dad, I got to go to a lot of church. I mean a lot, a lot. More church than any kid should probably know, but this was the early 90's, and we enjoyed going to church. It got to the point where my dad and I were a package deal. If my dad was preaching, I was singing The Lord's prayer before. In fact, I made my first $50 in life at six years old, singing for the funeral of a child. Looking back, I would reflect on how traumatic those experiences were—seeing the casket of a baby sitting on the front seat of a motorcade vehicle because it was too small to ride in the back cabin, not more than a wee bit bigger than a grasshopper myself, as they used to say. But even in the trauma of that scene, I cannot negate that on that day, like many previous and following occasions, my father would get to the house of the family early enough to pray with them. This may have just been his pastoral duty, but in my mind, my dad wouldn't meet them to pray at the church because he knew that on days as hard as this one, prayer must go before the people. It was like when he would pray, he wouldn't just ask God to comfort the family. He would pray that comfort would envelop them with every step they took. As if while he was praying, God was sending the words of his prayer like a legion of angel armies to pave the way for that family. From the house to the car, from the car to every street they took to the church, up every step, down the aisle. Back to the car, to every street, they would take to the cemetery. Literally, every step of the way.

These moments began to grow my understanding of the priority of prayer. They taught me that you could not have peace without prayer. If prayer was the first thing we do in times of difficulty, it became evident to me that prayer was sacred. It was a powerful thing that you pulled out to get through hardship and difficulty. That's when I began to understand prayer. Prayer began to formulate in the inner parts of my heart as a requirement. Like if we don't have anything else, we have prayer. Even my church breathed the DNA of prayer. Everything began and ended with prayer: Bible studies, rehearsals, tours, trips, family reunions, hospital visits, and home visits. Prayer was always present, preceding us. Prayer was shown to me throughout my life in practice, not theory. It wasn't just read about in the Bible that "men ought to always pray" (Luke 18:1); it was practiced, and that practice put us on track to the pilgrimage of prayer.

I'm not sure who you are reading this book or where you're from. I won't assume that you are of any specific demographic or background, but what I need you to know is that every black church in the 1990s was a family church. I don't care how big or small you were as a ministry. Black church in the 90's just hit differently. My childhood church was intimate for what we see in 2023. We comfortably saw about 450–600 people in our "hay day," and thousands came through. That was a lot of folks to know at that time. But church was fun, and everyone was one village. I came up in a day when other people in the church could discipline you as a child, and they weren't out of place because they would also bring you before your parents about it. It was community; it was covenant, one with another. Every family has their own traditions, and surely Mt. Calvary Free Will Baptist Church had theirs. In my opinion, if you came through Calvary, at some point you were going to have to participate in church. My youth pastor at the time, Dr. David E. Lanier iii was so on fire for God. Man "Mr. David" changed our lives. He was young, ambitious, brilliant, and full of the Holy Ghost! He took our little "Baptist" church to another level of fire. His methodology for ministry was one that was balanced with just as much church as we had fun. He ensured that there was always programming for us that fostered spiritual enrichment. One thing I could remember is the annual all-night prayer lock-ins, and for Calvary, this is the pilgrimage of young people. The year you were old enough to stay at church all night long with the big kids. My brother was 4 years older than me, and though he wasn't as into church as I was, he loved the community of friends he had there. So I would always want to get to that age where I, too, could stay at the all-night lock-in. I mean, I love church. Who wouldn't want to be there all night long? Not only did I love church, but church had the best food ever, and I wanted to go to church all night and wake up and eat this big breakfast there. Well, my year came, and my mom and dad finally let me stay. Little did I know this was the night Mr. David was going to make all of the young people pray. If you didn't know how to pray, you were going to learn that night. So, we are there on our knees, and everyone is just praying. My turn comes, and I didn't know what to pray for. Hundreds of young people are walking around calling on the name of Jesus and interceding. Some kneeled, some pacing the floor, and some laying prostrate. I hear Mr. David saying, "Just tell Him thank you." It seems simple, but in that moment, I felt like I didn't have to know how to speak in tongues yet. I didn't have to have all the depth of everyone around me; I just had to get there. I had to pilgrimage to that moment where I would experience being unafraid to talk to God in my own way. So I started telling Him thank you for the clothes on my back, the shoes on my feet, and the and the food on my table. Didn't even know what it meant, but I had heard my mama often say, "When I arose this morning, thank you that I was clothed in my right mind." I soon found out the real pilgrimage wasn't just about your moment to lead in prayer, but it was about learning the language of prayer. Believe it or not, the language is much simpler than some people may know.

WHAT IS PRAYER?

Let's talk about what prayer is and maybe a bit about what prayer isn't. Have you ever felt like you weren't equipped to pray? Like, if this were your younger self and someone asked you to lead the prayer in your congregation or community, you'd be readily available? Or maybe even your current self: do you shy away from moments of personal prayer or being a prayer leader in your congregation or community because you feel like what you have to say doesn't sound as "deep" or "wonderful" as something you've heard before? Well, if that's you, you don't know what prayer is. Because prayer, by definition, is "a solemn request for help or expression of thanks addressed to God, it's that simple. It's a fervent, unrelenting, unceasing hope. It is something that cannot be touched and cannot be taken because it is innately within your soul. That's what prayer is: the soul's desire, spoken and articulated before the Lord in communion with Him. When you pray, you show that you believe. Prayer is laced with belief at its foundation. The two terms are not mutually exclusive; you can't have one without the other. So the premise of prayer is derived from faith, even when you don't know faith is present. Prayer isn't something you have to pay for or conjure up. It's just something you must be willing to converse about with God.

THE IMPORTANCE OF PRAYER

Prayer is essential to a healthy and effective relationship with God. In today's world riddled with oppression, terrorism, political unrest, and family crises, every single day, the practice of prayer holds immense significance for the 21st-century believer. It helps us to not only anchor our soul but also our relationships. Think about it: communication is key to any successful relationship.

Effective communication is vital for fostering strong connections, whether they are romantic, platonic, or professional in nature. It is only communication that becomes the bridge that connects individuals. It is through communication that individuals can express their thoughts, emotions, and desires. By building open and honest communication, people are able to cultivate trust, deepen understanding, and nurture emotional intimacy. However, the key understanding is that it takes time to build effective communication. Effective communication is established in time! To be able to fully, completely, and in an uninterrupted fashion, without fear of judgement, not just for your actions but for your words. That's effective communication. Effective communication fosters an environment where people can openly express their vulnerabilities, fears, and desires. The good news is that you have an active and effective listener in God on the other end. Through the practice of active listening, empathy, and validation, partners can cultivate stronger connections and deepen their bonds. To experience being listened to brings a sense of appreciation in relationships and tends to foster feelings of security and emotional connection. But to know if your partner hears you, you must first trust them implicitly.

Effective communication allows individuals to handle conflicts and differences in a positive way. Have you ever noticed that the more you talk to a person, the easier it is to manage disagreements? Here's the reality: you won't always agree with every season and situation God allows you to experience in life. However, through open and respectful communication, we can effectively address any concerns we may carry. Through meditation and intentionality, when we give God time to speak back to us, we can discover shared perspectives and collaboratively seek resolutions. Effective communication plays a crucial role in fostering intimacy between people, as it necessitates openness, compassion, and shared comprehension. When people communicate with genuine and heartfelt sincerity, they can foster a deep emotional connection that enhances their relationship and maintains their bond over time.

Such is in a spiritual relationship with God, communication takes on a unique and profound significance. Just as effective communication is key to building intimacy between partners, communicating with God is essential for nurturing a deep and meaningful connection with God, who is fully spirit and fully the "I AM." Meaning God is not just Father, God is also a mother, helper, keeper, friend, brother, and sister. Prayer and meditation are essential for establishing a deep connection with God. Prayer allows us to openly communicate our gratitude, fears, hopes, and desires to an even greater power than we can imagine. Through prayer, we can foster a deep sense of faith and humility, recognizing the significance of our prayers and their reception by GOD. To pray in and of itself is an act of faith. As prayer speaks to belief, hope, and optimism. To pray would indicate that one has at least a glimmer of faith deep down on the inside of their soul.

THAT'S ALL YOU NEED (THE MATTHEW 17:14-21 LESSON)

"Then the disciples came to Jesus privately and asked, "Why could we not drive it out?" 20 He answered, "Because of your little faith [your lack of trust and confidence in the power of God]; for I assure you and most solemnly say to you, [a]if you have [living] faith the size of a mustard seed, you will say to this mountain, 'Move from here to there,' and [if it is God's will] it will move; and nothing will be impossible for you. 21 [But this kind of demon does not go out except by prayer and fasting.]" (Matthew 17:19–21 (AMP)," n.d.)

Do you know that 'The Morning Cup' is so important to me? Because it's all I need! Sometimes the practice of religion makes us feel totally unqualified to communicate our thoughts to God. As if we have to know the whole Bible to pray. Nope, maybe you need to pray to get the discipline to read the whole Bible. But do you know what your prayer shows? Faith! That's what! It shows desire, pursuit, and heart. That's what God is looking for, and that's enough. In Matthew 17:14–21, we see Jesus address His disciples after they were unable to heal a boy with a demon. When we read this scripture, we find that as soon as the possessed boy's father told Jesus that the disciples were unable to heal the boy, Jesus rebuked them for a lack of faith. Jesus shows us that when we lack faith, we fail to see miracles. That faith must be present for transformation to take place. The key thing to know, however, is that trying to have faith and having faith are two different things and produce two different results. Faking faith will keep you bound, while true faith releases us into the liberation of God's freedom that He has already provided for us. Maybe some of the victories you have expected to see by now haven't happened yet because you have been faking faith. Having a form of faith, the persona of faith, but deep in your heart you lack the belief it takes to see the miracles of God in your life. Well, these prayers are signed to help you cultivate an authentic hope through practical prayers. Jesus tells them that with faith the size of a mustard seed, they can move mountains. I am urging you to begin each day with words that aim to cultivate faith capable of moving mountains.

Faith that stands in the face of previous disappointments, believing that it is not the end, because as long as you can reach heaven on your knees, there is hope for your heart and help for your hands.

This is why prayer is important to us, but not just some prayer; avid prayers. Prayers that go without ceasing because even when they aren't on the surface of our lips, they exist in the inner recesses of our hearts. Prayer and meditation provide a space for intimate communication with God, allowing us to listen for divine guidance, wisdom, and presence. In this quiet reflection, we can develop a deeper awareness of God's love and compassion by growing a sense of intimacy and connection with God. Just as effective communication in relationships, one to another, involves vulnerability, empathy, and understanding, communication with God requires a similar level of openness and receptivity. By approaching prayer with sincerity, humility, and faith, we can create a sacred space for communion with God, deepening our spiritual connection and experiencing the transformative power of God's divine love for us. Communication in a spiritual relationship with God is a sacred exchange that nourishes the soul, fosters intimacy, and strengthens one's faith.

THE SIGNIFICANCE OF MORNING

“Very early in the morning, while it was still dark, Jesus got up, left the house, and went off to a solitary place, where he prayed."

-Mark 1:35 NIV

In Mark 1:35, Jesus wakes up early in the morning while it is still dark to go to a solitary place to pray. Solitude suggests that Jesus retreated to a place where He could hone His spirit and focus. This is similar to a place of meditation, a place where one's thoughts are deeply and intentionally focused on their relationship with God. The place where you shut out the noise and focus on the direction. This verse highlights the importance of starting the day with prayer and seeking solitude to connect with God. If Jesus Himself had to still a moment to remove himself from friends, followers, and fans, wouldn’t we too be subject to the need to prioritize and compartmentalize our relationship? Jesus understands the importance of intentional time. What better time than the morning? The morning time in the Bible is often associated with renewal, guidance, and preparing oneself for the day or journey ahead. It is seen as a sacred time to seek God's presence, wisdom, and strength for the challenges that may arise. The morning is a sign of newness! The morning brings with it new life, joy, hope, grace, and mercy. The Lord's loving kindness keeps us untouched, as His tender compassions never falter. 23 They are new every morning; great and beyond measure is Your faithfulness." ("Lamentations 3:22–23 (AMP)," n.d.) The morning comes with a spirit of refreshing. Sometimes all you have to do is convince yourself to make it until the morning. 12:01 AM every single day is the start of a new day, and the good thing is that it is not the light that defines the morning. In fact, morning is the period between midnight and noon. You don't even have to see the light to have proof that God is doing a new thing! It is, rather, the point of breaking. It is when the day that was must be no more and the day that is must come through. Whatever you are facing in the night season of your life must one day take its bow to the new beginning that God provides every single day. So the morning is essential to your faith because, like the day, it must be renewed. To renew your faith, is to daily decide to align before you ascend. Before you fix yourself to do anything else, have you given yourself a moment to commune with the giver of this new day? That's why I choose the morning cup; it has helped me to renew my faith daily with words of inspiration, affirmation, elevation, and meditation. By rising early in the morning to pray, Jesus sets an example for believers to prioritize spiritual communion with God at the beginning of each day. The quietness and stillness of the morning hours provide an opportunity for deeper reflection, focus, and listening to God's voice. Ultimately, we must seek God's presence and align our hearts and minds with His will while giving way to His voice.

GIVE WAY TO GOD'S VOICE.

I went to the dentist a few months ago, and she said to me, "Marissa I want you to use one toothpaste in the morning and a different one at night. But, when you're done, do not drink or rinse for at least 30 minutes." In my quest to understand why, she said, "Most people rinse their toothpaste thinking it's the proper way to brush, but when you rinse it immediately, you rinse away all the ingredients that are designed to strengthen your dental health." Welp, it was that moment when I realized that for 30+ years I had been missing all the good stuff because I was rinsing it away. Do you know that sometimes that's what we do with God? After we have our morning routine, we rinse off the good stuff by rushing into our day. Jumping straight into space with other people who bring a variety of energy. Sometimes you've got to give God a moment to speak back to you before you rinse. Sometimes you've got to keep the noise blocked out for just a bit longer to allow God space to actually answer you back. Sometimes we feel like our prayers are ineffective because we are looking for God to hit that reset button on the Nintendo joystick of our lives and just give us a new go. Sometimes giving God's voice a chance is just getting in your car and riding with your worship music and letting the lyrics of the song strengthen your heart. The key is that it is just as important to give God your time as it is to make an audience with Him for His.

Look at the words found in Jeremiah 29:12–13. "Then you will call on Me, and you will come and pray to Me, and I will hear [your voice] and I will listen to you. 13 Then [with a deep longing], you will seek Me and require Me [as a vital necessity], and you will find Me when you search for Me with all your heart." (Jeremiah 29:12–13 (AMP)," n.d.) In this moment, the prophet is giving the word of the Lord to those who are exiled in Babylon: "You will pray, and I will hear your voice." Although the children of Israel are facing the turmoil and bondage of being exiled into the literal representation of sin and captivity, God sends them a word that, at the appointed time, I will hear your voice and I will also listen to you. Because God is our father, mother, and creator, God is listening to our voices and our cries and concerns. He even invites us to bring to Him what burdens us, and He will "give us rest" (Matthew 11:28). We must be intentional about hearing from God as well as surrendering to God. Prayer serves as a powerful tool that can provide comfort, clarity, and resilience in the face of such overwhelming challenges.

PRAY FOR TODAY

In the midst of difficulties, prayer can provide solace, healing, and renewal. It offers a platform for us to openly share our fears, worries, and aspirations and to find comfort and resilience during challenging and uncertain times. By seeking relief in prayer, we can discover the strength and connection necessary to overcome life's challenges and emerge with strength you can only get in the war room. The relevance of prayer for believers in the 21st century cannot be overstated, especially in the face of the challenges this current climate brings. Prayer is an effective strategy that enables us to face challenges with bravery, humanity, and strength. It serves as a source of hope, giving direction and refuge to those who seek Him because He has availed Himself to be found, according to Jeremiah 29:13.

In this day and age, prayer is more essential than ever. Every day, there is some new challenge to grapple with, some new trouble to face, and some new test to overcome. The places that our problems span aren't just personal but global. While we are always concerned with praying for and covering our house, we also have to pray for the things that go on in the White House. The things that end up on the Senate floor and the issues on Capitol Hill. We must pray for the war that is going on in Gaza and the restoration of the faith of the community of individuals affected by the tragedies there. We must pray for the generation who will be exposed to television programming that is less censored now than ever before and an internet that, on any given day, can bust Hell wide open if this were an apostolic World Wide Web. In fact, I take that back; 2024's internet is a little too 'gangsta' for the Baptists too. Either way, you get my drift. We gotta stay prayed up! Because Amalek is on the attack.

I am reminded of this story in Exodus Chapter 17, where the Children of Israel are wandering without water and frustrated with their leader, Moses. But their struggle with transition and their frustration with their disposition didn't stop Amalek from showing up there in the valley in Rephidem. They were frustrated, tired, overwhelmed, overworked, and wandering without water, but the enemy didn't let up. Do you know that every day we are fighting an enemy that doesn't let up the pressure? I'm talking about the enemies of depression: defeat, distress, disillusionment, dismay, and discomfort. There are a lot of enemies, and we are at war. So this is why we cannot negate the necessity of daily seeking the Lord. When you finish this 21-day cycle, you may find yourself in another cycle that may require another level of dedication and that may help you develop a new perspective. Just pray for the day—every day! Pray with accuracy and clarity. Pray without shame and with vulnerability. Pray for exactly what you need from God. Pray from different angles of prayer. Prayer of intercession, thanksgiving, supplication, adoration, meditation, comfort, etc. Just pray, knowing God is listening and, there is always an enemy lurking. So, while I've done my best to be political and polite, when it comes to 2024, "you've got to keep your head on a swivel." IN HIM.

DAY 1: A PRAYER OF SALVATION.

This prayer of salvation must be day one of this spiritual journey. Salvation is not only a priority for spirituality but is also a prerequisite for accessing the presence of God. When you come into salvation with Jesus Christ, you welcome Him into your life and heart to operate as your redeemer from the penalty of sin. But you know what? It's possible to be so saved that you forget that your salvation also needs some maintenance, so maybe today's prayer isn't directly for you, but you too can pray this prayer for yourself or introduce someone else to this prayer. If you are praying this for the first time and you're alone, don't worry! Imagine me as your prayer B.F.F. (Best Friend Forever), celebrating your decision to give your life over to Jesus Christ. When you pray this prayer with belief in your heart, God does the rest! Ready? Let's pray...

God, today I want to thank you for the gift of salvation! Thank you that it is full and free! Thank you; that is complete and enough! Thank you that even after everything I have done and seen in my life, your saving grace is still reaching out to me. So, God, today I ask that you would come into my heart. Regardless of how many times I have or have not prayed this prayer, today, again and forever more, I accept that I am a sinner in need of a savior, that I am dead in you, but desire to come alive through the grace and power of your resurrection. So today, God, I believe in my heart that you are the only begotten son of God, and that you died on the cross, was crucified, dead, and buried, but on the third day arose with all power in your hand! So because you have this power and have extended this power to us, I confess you as the Lord and leader of my life, my soul, my thoughts, my intentions, and my plans! Make me new today, wash me over, and I confess by faith that I am saved! In Jesus name, Amen.

DAY 2: A PRAYER OF PEACE,

On day two of this spiritual journey, I would like to help you develop a prayer for peace. Having peace means having the power to have tranquility in times of tribulation. Every single day, this world brings us things that can feel like tribulation to our soul. Heartache, grief, rejection—just the woes of the world. It's hard to keep your "head above water" in the midst of all of that. Peace is crucial for our mental and emotional well-being, physical health, relationships with others and God, productivity and creativity, and spiritual growth. When we have peace, we are liberated to be our best selves. That is why we pray for peace. So that we can stabilize our spirits and seek God without distractions. You ready? Let's pray....

God, today We come before you perhaps with heavy hearts or heavy hands longing for the peace that only you can provide. In a world filled with chaos, violence, and uncertainty today, we seek your presence to calm our fears and bring us help and strength.

God, today I ask that you would grant me the wisdom to seek peaceful resolutions. In every area where tension may exist in my life, I ask for the courage to stand up against injustice. I also ask that you would give me compassion to love my neighbors as myself. Help me to be peacemakers in our words and actions, spreading your love and grace wherever you have ordained for me to be today.

May your peace, which surpasses all understanding, safeguard my heart and mind in Christ Jesus. In the midst of turmoil, I choose to believe you for the blessings of your promises and strength in your presence.

I pray for peace in my home, my community, this nation, and this world. Let your peace reign in every corner of the earth and cover every inch of my soul, so that I may serve you wholly! In Jesus' name, amen

DAY 3: A PRAYER FOR FAITH.

On day three of this spiritual journey, I would like to help you develop a prayer for faith. Faith is not just our foundation. It is our anchor. Without it, we have nothing. "Faith, according to the word of God, is the substance of things hoped for and the evidence of things unseen." In other words, faith is the proof that you believe in what you cannot see. Now, if I can pray for what I can't see, certainly I can certainly experience it. This is why we need faith—to believe that miracles are moving behind our prayers. To believe that when we pray, God causes the entire universe to start taking flight around His word to meet you in your future! So today we pray this prayer of faith. Are you ready? Let's pray....

God, Today I come before you with a humbled heart, seeking to strengthen my faith in you. You are the source of all strength, wisdom, and power, and I acknowledge my need for a stronger and more unwavering faith. God daily, there are troubles and trials that challenge my belief, but today I ask for more of you.

Help me to trust you more fully, to surrender my doubts and fears, and to hold fast to your word even in the midst of uncertainties. Strengthen my faith and renew my hope in your goodness and faithfulness.

Grant me the courage to step out in faith, to take risks for your kingdom, and to walk boldly in the path you have set before me. May my faith be a light that shines in the darkness, a beacon of hope and truth in a world filled with doubt and despair.

As I navigate the challenges of life, I ask that you deepen my trust in your provision, your protection, and your guidance. Help me to seek your will above all else, to listen for your voice in the quiet moments, and to follow where you lead with unwavering obedience.

Lord, I ask for a faith that moves mountains, a faith that conquers fear, and a faith that never wavers in the face of adversity. Fill me with your Holy Spirit, empower me to live out my faith boldly, and help me to be a living testimony of your grace and love to those around me.

Thank you, Lord, for the gift of faith and for the assurance that you are with me always. Strengthen my faith, Lord, and help me to walk in confidence and trust in you each day.

In Jesus' name, I pray, amen.

DAY 4: A PRAYER FOR HOPE.

On day four of this spiritual journey, I would like to help you develop a prayer for hope. When I think of having hope, I am reminded of the prophet Jeremiah, who in Lamentations says, "This I recall to my mind; therefore, have I hope; it is of the Lord's mercies that we are not consumed" ("Lamentations 3:21–24 (NIV)," n.d.). Jeremiah had a unique ability to be able to find the beauty in the burden. He says I have hope because I realize that, as bad as it could be, it hasn't overtaken me. That's mercy, and it is found in renewing our hope. It's found in asking God to strengthen and make our hope better and more anchored in Him. Sometimes you have to examine your history to have hope for your tomorrow. Jeremiah says, "I have found hope in reflecting on the fact that things could possibly be worse than this." So today, as we pray for hope, I pray that you find an anchor to the God of your hope. Are you ready? Let's pray....

God, today I want to thank you for the blessing of a new day that gives me hope to believe that a new day is coming. Thank you. In times of darkness and uncertainty, you are our source of hope and strength. You are the light that guides us through the darkness, the anchor that holds us steady in the storm. When all seems lost, you remind us that hope is never far away.

Today, I ask that you give me the courage to face every challenge with faith and perseverance, knowing that you are always by my side. Help me to trust in your promises and to cling to the hope that is found in your unfailing love.

I ask that your presence fill me with peace and assurance, casting out every trace of doubt and fear. Rekindle the flame of hope within my heart, reminding me that with you, all things are possible.

I pray for those who are struggling to find hope in the midst of despair. May your light radiate upon them, bringing comfort, strength, and a renewed sense of purpose. Help us to be instruments of hope in the lives of others, sharing your love and grace wherever we go.

Thank you, Lord, for being my constant source of hope and assurance. May I go through this day knowing that you hold my future in your hands and that your plans for me are good. In Jesus' name, I pray, amen.

DAY 5: A PRAYER FOR PERSPECTIVE.

On day five of this spiritual journey, I would like to help you develop a prayer for perspective. Having a good perspective is essential in life, as it allows you to see things in a broader context and seek understanding in all things. It helps us to cultivate gratitude, resilience, and compassion towards ourselves and others. With a positive and spiritual perspective, we are able to find peace, purpose, and contentment in trouble. When we shift perspective from negativity to positivity, we can transform our outlook on life and adopt a more hopeful and empowered mindset. This enables us to let go of unnecessary worries and fears, trusting that God is guiding our journey. Having a good perspective provides us with clarity, faith, and wisdom to navigate life's challenges with grace and humility. It fosters growth, healing, and spiritual development, leading you towards a path of self-discovery, enlightenment, and inner peace, so let's pray today. Are you ready? Let's pray...

God, today I come before you seeking a perspective that mirrors Your divine wisdom, grace, and will for my life. I recognize that life and death is in the power of my tongue, so God, today, help me to speak from a place of grace, faith, and hope.

I ask that you would give me the strength and clarity to shift my perspective from whatever negativity may be trying to overtake my space and my spirit to the positivity of your power and peace, that makes every spirit of negativity bow. I ask that you cause Your light to illuminate my way and infuse my heart with hope and empowerment. God, guide me to release unnecessary worries and fears, trusting wholeheartedly in Your guiding hand and unwavering love.

Help me, Lord, to view life's challenges as opportunities for growth, healing, and spiritual development. May my perspective be a beacon of light, leading me towards self-discovery, enlightenment, and inner peace in Your presence. Let my outlook be one of grace and humility, reflecting Your wisdom and boundless love.

Today, I surrender my heart and mind to You, inviting Your transformative power to shape my perspective and align it with Your divine purpose. Help me to see things from a place of victory. Help me to walk in faith, guided by Your eternal truth. Help me to find solace and strength in knowing that Your presence is always with me. In Jesus name, amen.

DAY 6: A PRAYER FOR GOALS.

On day six of this spiritual journey, I would like to help you develop a prayer for your goals. Goals are important to us. But one of our greatest downfalls is that we often don't ensure our goals align with what God wants for us. When we pray, we must ensure that we ask God for His will to override our desire. When we pray for our goals, we pray that God would give us the inspiration, motivation, and creativity to dream and envision according to His ever-evolving, unfolding plan in our lives. As we navigate through the seasons and decades of our lives, we must be willing to relinquish our plans to His. So as we pray today, let's pray for goals that align with God's will for our lives. Are you ready? Let's pray....

God, today I come before you with my heart open and humble. I acknowledge that the goals I have for my life are important to me, but I also recognize the significance of aligning them with Your divine will. So today, God, I ask that you would help me, to seek Your guidance and wisdom as I set my aspirations and dreams. God, give my spirit the grace to discern your direction for my dreams!

I ask that you would give me the inspiration to dream big, the motivation to persevere, and the creativity to envision a future that reflects Your eternal plan for my life. Teach me to surrender my desires and plans to Your higher purpose, trusting in Your perfect timing and wisdom in all things.

As I navigate through the seasons of life, may my goals be in alignment with Your will, guiding me towards growth, service, and spiritual fulfillment. Give me the strength to relinquish my agenda and embrace Your unfolding plan with faith and surrender.

May my prayers for goals be rooted in Your love, fueled by Your grace, and aligned with Your divine purpose for me. Today, I place my dreams and ambitions in Your hands, knowing that Your will surpasses all understanding and leads me to abundant blessings. In Jesus name, amen.

DAY 7: A PRAYER FOR FAMILY.

On day seven of this spiritual journey, I would like to help you develop a prayer for your family. Praying for your family is a critical part of our responsibility as intercessors. We are called to "stand in the gap for" those we love and lead. Praying for and even with our families deepens our connection with each other and fosters a sense of unity, love, and support within the family unit. It is important to develop practical and pragmatic prayers for your family to strengthen spiritual bonds and spiritual fortitude. Prayers for our family should include, but aren't limited to, things such as asking God for their spiritual growth and guidance. Seeking unity and harmony within the walls of your home and the bonds of your bloodline. Praying for emotional strength, healthy communication, and more. Praying with family helps the house! You know the old saying, "The family that prays together stays together." Are you ready? Let's pray...

God, today I come before You with a heart of gratitude and love for the blessing of family. Even if everything isn't ideal, thank you that you have sent systems of surroundings and support into my life. Today I acknowledge that I need your guidance and grace in leading and loving my family. So today, I stand in the gap on their behalf and on behalf of my house. Today I ask that you fortify our bonds and strengthen our spirituality. I pray that in whatever areas anyone in my house is lacking in their lives, your divine intervention will come and shift them to a new level in you.

Today I pray for the growth and guidance of everyone in my house and in my heart. I pray that your light will shine into every dark place they may be facing and deliver them from any place that the enemy has them bound. Today, I pray against attack, retaliation, confusion, crisis, and predatory behaviors. I pray that no plague will come nigh, their dwelling place. I ask that you give each member of my family more wisdom, discernment, and a deepening faith that will guide their steps and decisions each day.

I ask that you make my home harmonious and cause unity to reign within our walls. Help us to cultivate a spirit of love, forgiveness, and understanding that transcends any conflict or discord, binding us together in Your divine peace and grace.

Bless us with emotional strength to navigate life's challenges, and give us the gift of healthy communication that fosters understanding, empathy, and mutual support. May our words be filled with kindness, our actions with compassion, and our hearts with humility as we interact with one another.

Thank You, Lord, for the gift of family and the opportunity to pray. Fortify and strengthen the spiritual bonds that unite us, anchoring us in Your love and grace. May our family be a beacon of light and hope to others and a testament to the power of faith and unity in Your name. In Jesus' name, amen.

DAY 8: A PRAYER FOR INCREASE & OVERFLOW.

On day eight of this spiritual journey, I would like to help you develop a prayer for increase and overflow. Life has a funny way of making you feel like you are constantly losing or cycling things out. If not things, perhaps people, maybe resources. All in all, it is easy to feel depleted by the natural goings and comings of life. This is a prayer for abundance, increase, overflow, and harvest. This prayer is designed to be a mantra of affirmation over not just your day but your life. Believing that God's word is just as relevant over your life as it was to David when he penned this psalm, "For the Lord God is a sun and shield; The Lord bestows grace and favor and honor; No good thing will He withhold from those who walk uprightly." ("Psalm 84:11 (AMP)," n.d.) Are you ready? Let's pray....

God, I come before you with a heart full of gratitude for all the blessings you have given me. I thank you for the resources and opportunities you have provided to me thus far and all the ones you have stored for my future. Today, I lift up every need that exists within my life before you, but I also raise to you my aspirations.

Today, I pray for an increase and overflow in my finances, business, and wealth. I ask that you open doors of opportunity, grant me wisdom and discernment in my financial decisions, and bless the work of my hands. May your favor and abundance surround me, lead to prosperity, and cause me to experience success in all that I do.

Help me, God, to be a good steward of the resources you entrust to me. Help me use them wisely for the greater good and the advancement of your kingdom and my community. Teach me to be generous in my giving and disciplined in my living. Teach me how to share my blessings with others, embodying the spirit of abundance and gratitude.

Today, I also pray for financial breakthroughs and new avenues for growth and prosperity. Lead me to opportunities that align with your will, purpose, and prosperity for my life. God guide me in making sound financial choices that honor you.

Thank you, Lord, for your provision, your faithfulness, and your promise to meet all our needs according to your riches in Christ Jesus. I trust in your timing and your plan for my holistic well-being and my future. Knowing that you are God, who rewards those who seek you diligently. In Jesus' name, amen.

DAY 9: A PRAYER FOR HEALING.

On day nine of this spiritual journey, I would like to help you develop a prayer for healing. It is vital that we eliminate thoughts of doubt and fear when we are facing situations such as sickness or brokenness of the mind, body, or spirit. When we pray for healing, we seek a sense of hope, positivity, and inner strength that can positively impact our physical, emotional, and spiritual well-being. There is a connection between mind and body that is validated in Proverbs 23:7. "For as a person thinks, in their heart, so are they." Meaning there is a spiritual connection between mind and body that allows us to know we can will ourselves into more positive spaces if we just put our faith into action. Prayers for healing give us a positive outlook, which translates to emotional support. It causes us to see miracles and interventions, as well as find purpose and meaning in times of trouble. When we pray and give God's voice room to speak back to us, we allow Him the space to settle us and find the comfort to trust His will. Praying for healing will give us a positive perspective, give us support for our souls, and help us find purpose even in the pits of life. Are you ready? Let's pray...

God, today I come seeking your healing power to flow in my life! Today, through faith, I claim that the power that you have made available to heal and make us whole is flowing through my environment. You are the Great Physician, the source of all healing and comfort. So today, I place my trust in you and ask for your mercy and grace to bring healing to my body, mind, and soul.

As you begin moving on my request, I ask that you eliminate the places where pain exists, not just in my body but in my heart and mind. God, I ask that you bring restoration, wholeness, and drive out all residue of infirmity from me. God, today I ask that you make me a miracle in this earth. That you would cause your healing power to be shown in me so that I may testify that you are able to do exceeding and abundant things in our lives.

Today I surrender my worries, fears, stresses, and every point of doubt in my life to give you full control. Today, help me to see that even in the face of pain, you are a healer and mind regulator. Today, while I pray for my healing, I ask that you heal those around me who are standing in need. I pray that your healing presence will be felt by all who are sick or hurting, bringing comfort, peace, and restoration to their lives. I give you thanks now, believing that you have already heard me and sent help for me. In Jesus' name, amen.

DAY 10: A PRAYER FOR BREAKTHROUGH.

On day ten of this spiritual journey, I would like to help you develop a prayer for breakthrough. A spiritual breakthrough is a transformative experience or realization that leads to a deepened connection with God and oneself. It is what leads us to a greater sense of purpose and meaning in life. A breakthrough often involves a profound shift in consciousness, beliefs, or understanding that opens up new possibilities for growth, healing, and spiritual development. A spiritual breakthrough can bring clarity, insight, and inspiration, leading to a heightened sense of awareness, peace, and alignment with our inner truth and values. It can be a moment of profound revelation, inner healing, or spiritual awakening that propels an individual towards personal transformation, enlightenment, and a deeper connection with God. When we pray for breakthroughs, we cancel out breakdowns and burnouts. A breakthrough is a prayer of belief that a shift will happen suddenly! Today, as you pray for breakthrough, imagine God taking the strength of His authority and shattering the chains of every situation that has you captive, mentally, spiritually, or relationally. Are you ready? Let's pray...

God, today I want to thank you for this place I am in at this very moment. Even if this place isn't comfortable for me, I want to thank you because I'm still on my feet. God, at this moment, in the midst of whatever weariness and weakness that exists around me, I come seeking you for complete and total breakthrough. God, today I believe that just as you have done throughout the days of your word, you are the God who brings us victory in the face of defeat, so today I am believing you for intervention in every issue I am up against.

God, today I come to lay my burdens before you, asking that you take every challenge and struggle that has depleted me and reverse it in my favor. Cause a divine turn-around that would cause every place of defeat to relent. God, today I pray that you would transform every part of me that is not aligned with breakthrough. So that even if I am my own hinderance, you can break me for breakthrough.

Today I ask that you grant me the strength to face the obstacles that stand in my way, the courage to confront my fears, and the faith to believe in the possibility of breakthrough and liberation from the bonds that have held me captive. Infuse me with Your strength, Your love, and Your healing grace that renews my soul.

Lord, I surrender my worries, my doubts, and my weariness at Your feet, trusting in Your infinite wisdom and mercy to guide me towards a path of restoration and renewal. Break through the barriers that confine me, the doubts that paralyze me, and the fears that hinder me! Free me to walk in the fullness of Your love and purpose for my life.

Today, let Your spirit dwell within me! Comfort me in times of distress, empower me in moments of weakness, and lead me towards a place of peace, joy, and spiritual abundance. Give me the breakthrough today, O Lord, that I may rise above the struggles that surround me and emerge stronger, wiser, and more aligned with Your divine will for my life. In Jesus name, Amen.

DAY 11: A PRAYER FOR THE NEXT GENERATION

On day eleven of this spiritual journey I would like to help you develop a prayer for our youth. Praying for the next generation of believers is critical to the continuity of Christianity. But specifically during this day and time, covering youth at this crucial stage of their lives is extremely important. Through prayer, we can seek God so that they can find the guidance, strength, and clarity they need to overcome the obstacles they face during adolescence and young adulthood. When we pray for our youth, we seek God for their spiritual guidance, clarity and discernment, strength and resilience, protection and guidance, direction, and purpose. Most importantly truth and light, we pray that God would place a hedge of protection over them so that they can bear witness to the works of God for generations to come. So when we pray today, let's lift up the next generation all over this world. You could be praying for the answer to the very issues you've been facing! Are you ready? Let's pray....

God today, lift up the next generation and the youth of this nation to you, especially those who are minorities and at risk. You know each one by name, and you see their struggles, their challenges, and their potential. I pray for your protection, guidance, and provision for their lives.

For those who face discrimination, prejudice, and injustice, I ask that you would give them the strength to stand tall in the face of adversity. Help them to overcome obstacles and to believe in their worth and dignity as your children.

For those who are at risk of poverty, violence, addiction, or hopelessness, surround them with your love and grace. Provide them with positive role models, safe environments, and opportunities for growth and transformation.

I ask that your Spirit empower this generation of seekers to find you, to rise above their circumstances, to dream big, and to pursue their passions with courage and determination. God, help them to discover their gifts, talents, and purpose in life and to use them for the betterment of themselves and their communities.

I pray for leaders and mentors to come alongside them to, offer support, encouragement, and resources to help them succeed. May the voices of the marginalized be heard, the needs of the vulnerable be met, and the futures of all youth be filled with hope and possibility.

Thank you, Lord, for your unfailing love and compassion toward the youth of this nation. May they know that they are valued, cherished, and deeply loved by you. In Jesus' name pray, amen.

DAY 12: A PRAYER FOR JOY.

On day twelve of this spiritual journey I would like to help you develop a prayer for Joy. It is essential to maintain a daily renewed joy in God to maintain a positive and adaptable mindset, even when faced with life's difficulties and uncertainties. When we purposefully develop a deep connection with God on a daily basis, we foster a profound appreciation, optimism, and peace that can provide reprieve during challenging moments. We must embrace the power of daily renewal to cultivate a profound connection with our faith, discover refuge in times of hardship, and uncover a true sense of purpose and fulfillment. Finding joy in God has the power to ignite acts of kindness, compassion, and love towards others, resulting in a ripple effect of positivity and goodness in our lives and the lives of those around us. In the end, when we make it a priority to find joy in God every day, we develop a resilient, grateful, and content spirit that can change how we see life and bring us lasting fulfillment and peace. When you pray today, ask for the goodness of God to renew your joy and grant you an unwavering sense of satisfaction that is unaltered by the chaos of the world. Pray as if you are receiving joy from God in return for all the chaos in this culture. Are you ready? Let's Pray...

God, today, in the midst of our trials and tribulations, I come before you seeking the restoration of our joy. Life's tumultuous tests can leave us feeling drained, weary, and devoid of happiness. But it is proven that in you, I can discover authentic and enduring joy that remains above any situation.

Today I ask that you pour out your presence upon me and replenish the well of joy within my heart. I ask that you would lift the burdens that weigh me down, remove the clouds of despair that obscure my vision, and renew my spirit with the light of your love.

Help me to find joy in the small moments of each day, to see the glory in your handiwork, and to appreciate the blessings that surround me. Give me the strength to let go of past hurts, to forgive those who have wronged me, and to embrace a spirit of gratitude and positivity.
I pray that my joy be rooted in you, so that it is not moved y every trial that blows my way. God, help me to trust in

your plans for my future, knowing that you are a God who brings restoration, redemption, and new beginnings.

Thank you, Lord, for being my source of joy and for turning my mourning into dancing. God, let me forever rejoice in your goodness, celebrate your faithfulness, and walk in the light of your love each day. In Jesus' name, I pray, amen.

DAY 13: A PRAYER FOR HELP.

On day thirteen of this spiritual journey, I would like to help you develop a prayer for help. When praying to God for help, I believe it is important that we approach God with humility, faith, and sincerity while asking for assistance. I believe it is important to ensure that our relationship with God is not transactional in nature but true in heart. It is important to emphasize that our priority and sincerity are always positioned towards authenticity to serve God wholly. So when we seek, we must first acknowledge His lordship and reign in our lives. We must be upfront and truthful about our desires and our motivations. It is important to search your heart for desires that are not more of a priority to you than they are to God. I believe we must be foremost about praise and appreciation of God. When we prove faithfulness with little, God blesses us with much. Most importantly, have the faith and desire to see His miracles more than your blessing. When you want to see His glory first, He will do it for His name sake! So today, pray for help with a heart of humility. Are you ready? Let's pray...

God, today I come to You asking for Your intervention and your help. Today I am asking You with a humbled heart, overflowing with faith, and a heartfelt cry for Your help. I am grateful for Your compassion and sovereignty, because I know that You are the source of all of my help and refuge. God, I acknowledge today how much better you have been to me throughout my life than I have been to myself. So today I come to You in humility, understanding my own limits and putting my faith in Your unlimited love and power as I lift up my heart to you. God, please help me to come to You with a real and sincere desire to seek Your will above all else. Help me to never handle my spirituality transactionally. God, I pray that integrity and truth be the foundation of our relationship, and that my highest priority is serving You completely. I ask that you give me the discernment to know what You want me to do, as well as the courage to follow in Your footsteps. I put my faith in Your perfect timing and unwavering love. I am thankful for Your constant presence and your commitment to help me when I am in need. So today, whatever the hindrance is, send your help. Help for my hurt, my shame, my lack, and my frustration. Please send your help, and I will thank praise you in the process. In Jesus' name, amen.

DAY 14: A PRAYER FOR COMFORT.

On day fourteen of this spiritual journey, I would like to help you develop a prayer for comfort. The word of God provides assurance that we have a comforter. " 26 "But when the [a] Helper (Comforter, Advocate, Intercessor—Counselor, Strengthener, Standby) comes, whom I will send to you from the Father, that is the Spirit of Truth who comes from the Father, He will testify and bear witness about Me." ("John 15:26 (AMP)," n.d.) To have the comforter with you would ensure that, regardless of the chaos of the moment, there is an aid by your side to bring you warmth and feelings of security in your discomfort. This is going to sound corny, and maybe I'll date myself here, but I remember being a young girl going to sleep in daycare at the 'Little Lambs daycare center'. I can remember when it was nap time and it was lights out bodies to the cots on the cold floor. At that time, it wasn't popular to have carpeted daycare centers, foam mats, and soothing sounds to sleep with, like my Sham, Sham is provided. Oh no! It was a little scary, but I remember when the time came to take my comforter for the week, I always wanted to take my barney blanket. There was something about that comforter that always allowed me to find peace, no matter how much I hated the situation.

That's what we have in God. A comforter, a place of familiarity that always does the trick. When we relinquish ourselves to the way He wants to comfort us, we allow God to invite us into peace that surpasses our understanding. Are you ready? Let's pray….

God, today I come to you acknowledging that there are times in my life where I am pulled into the pit of despair. Moments when I raise the questions that David raised in the Psalms, "Why art thou cast down, oh my soul? Why art thou disquieted within me?" God, but even in these unsettling moments of life, I know that you are with me. You are Emmanuel, and you will never abandon me. Today, God, I ask that you would be my comfort. I acknowledge that you are the God of all comfort, the God who invites us to release our burdens in times of distress. Today, I come before you, asking for your peace and presence to surround me wherever I may be.

Today, I pray that your healing touch will mend the hearts of those who are experiencing the physical loss of a loved one. Today, also pray for those who have faced the upsets of life that have left us comfortless. I pray that you will remind us of the hope we have in you. God, I ask that you comfort me today in every place where I have been without rest, and peace. God, even the places I have not confessed with my mouth, but cry with my heart. I ask that you restore and renew me.

Today, I pray for your wisdom, courage, and comfort in times of loss, change, and transition in their lives. Thank you for the peace of knowing that you are with us every step of the way. Today, please help me find comfort in knowing that you control my destiny and have a plan for my life.

Lord, today, I pray that your presence be an anchor directing us out of the depths and into the embrace of your love in the midst of our suffering. Please help me to find calm in the midst of life's uncertainties, strength in my shortcomings, and solace in your promises.

God, I am grateful that you are my rock, my sanctuary, and my peace of mind when I am in need. So today, I pray that your arms of kindness may envelop me and calm every place where I am worn out. Today I ask that you would comfort me to take rest in your plans. In Jesus' name, amen.

DAY 15: A PRAYER FOR RENEWAL.

On day fifteen of this spiritual journey, I would like to help you develop a prayer for renewal. Praying for renewal allows us to seek inner strength, peace, and guidance from God. It can help us reset our minds and hearts, especially during turbulent times. But when we pray, God brings us renewal in prayer. Prayer is the place of grounding and fortitude. That's why we do it at the beginning of the day. It is designed to give us what we need to sustain ourselves throughout the varying atmospheres we will encounter. Sometimes you don't even know what you're going to need. That's why you must be prayed up in the morning, so that you are not going into your day depleted. When we pray, we renew our spirits and relationships with God, deepening our connection with Him.

To renew a thing means to restore or make it whole. To make it well and back proper standing. Sometimes the heaviness around us weighs on our spirits, and sin downright disconnects us from God. But we need renewal to constantly be accountable to refreshing our relationships and our souls. In Psalm 51:10, David asks God to "create in me a clean heart, O God, and renew a right spirit within me." He asks God to revitalize his posture so that he can fulfill his purpose! Today, I pray that this prayer helps to revitalize your purpose! Are you ready? Let's pray...

God, today I come before You, seeking renewal in my spirits. In moments of weakness, I ask that you help find strength in Your presence, and power. In times of turmoil, I pray to find peace in Your guidance. Help me to reset my mind and heart, allowing Your light to shine through the darkness.

Lord, as I seek to deepen my relationship with You, I ask that you would create in me a clean heart and renew right spirit within me, just as David prayed in Psalm 51:10. I ask that you lead me to wholeness, make me well, and set me on the path of righteousness.

God, I acknowledge the heaviness that weighs on my spirit from time to time, and the ways in which sin can disconnect me from You. So today I repent of everything that hinders me from hearing you! God, I ask that you would grant me the grace to seek renewal, to be accountable for refreshing my relationship with You, and nurturing my soul through communion with You.

Today, I pray that this prayer will be a catalyst for revitalizing my purpose, and aligning me with Your will so that I may fulfill the calling You have placed on my life. Thank you for the gift of renewal and for your unending love and grace. In Jesus' name, amen.

DAY 16: A PRAYER FOR MINISTRY.

On day sixteen of this spiritual journey, I would like to help you develop a prayer for ministry. When praying, we pray for ministry; we must pray beyond ourselves. Not only do we pray for the ministries we are apart of, but we also pray for the success of ministries that are doing good, honest, life-building work in our communities. We also pray for the ministries that we have been given. The ministry of reconciliation. Our call to bringing the broken back to the God who is waiting for them to come to Him. Ministry is a serious thing. So when we pray, we much pray for wisdom and discernment, strength and endurance, spiritual growth, impact and effectiveness, protection, and provision. Certainly for opportunity and continuity. So when you pray today, think of the needs the ministry meets. Pray Gods will be one. Are you ready? Let's pray...

God, I come today to lift up ministries around the world in prayer. Today, I seek to pursue my call to serve as a minister to the lost and broken. So today, I pray for wisdom and discernment for all who do ministry for your people. I pray that you would give us the wisdom to make sound decisions and follow Your lead in every aspect of our work.

God, give I ask for strength and endurance to all ministers, volunteers, and ministry workers. That they may persevere through challenges and remain steadfast in their service to others. May Your power sustain them as they carry out the tasks set before them.

God, I pray for unity and peace within ministries so that team members, volunteers, and the community can come together in one accord, working towards common goals and building strong relationships rooted in Your love.

I ask that you nurture us in the spirit and continue to deepen our faith and relationship with You. God, let our service be a means of drawing closer to You and growing in grace.

I pray for the impact and effectiveness of the ministries that you have given purpose to, for this season. That lives may be touched, hearts may be transformed, and Your kingdom may be advanced through ministry efforts. I pray that every action be taken to bring glory to Your name.

God, we also ask for Your protection and provision. Keep leaders, volunteers, and those being served safe, and provide resources for the meeting of all their needs, both material and spiritual.

Open doors for new opportunities to reach more people, share Your message, and make a difference in the community through ministries. Stir hearts, open minds, and lead many to encounter Your love through their work. In Jesus' name, amen.

DAY 17: A PRAYER FOR CAREERS.

On day seventeen of this spiritual journey, I would like to help you develop a prayer for careers. When we pray for effective career paths that fulfill God's purpose, we should focus our prayers on direction and discernment; to be in God-ordained spaces in our lives. We must also pray for passion and calling to ensure that we are led towards places of purpose. When we pray, we ask God to open doors in our favor, equip us with the necessary skills and abilities for success, and enable us to make an impact and influence. When we pray for these key areas, we can seek God's direction and blessings as we pursue effective career paths and successes that align with His plans for our lives.

Often, we find ourselves cycling through seasons of frustration when it feels like we are ready for new levels in our lives. But all we see is more of the same, and feel stuck and stagnant. Well, maybe the problem is that you are praying for change when we should be asking for new networks. Because perhaps what God wants to do in your next season is not behind a door you've already seen before. You've got to pray for direction and discernment. Because maybe fear is keeping your request too small.

When you pray today, I challenge you to believe God, that your next move will be your best move! Are you ready? Let's pray...

God, today I come before you to lift up my aspirations in prayer. Today I am asking for Your guidance and wisdom in every step that I take. God, I pray that you would give me the discernment needed to understand Your will for my life and to make decisions that align with Your purpose. God, I have seen what my plans and powers produce. In this season, I want to prioritize seeing your plan and your power. I pray that you would cause your ideas for my life to innovate my path and your creativity to light my way. God, I submit my plans for you today! I ask that you would guide me into doors of opportunity, open up networks of favor, and guide me in every decision I make.

I pray that you would help me to prioritize my relationship with you, my family, and my personal well-being. Help me to plan and strategize according to the favor you have ordained for my faith to see. God, show me my passions and calling according to your desire for my life. I ask that you would equip me with the skills and abilities needed to excel in my chosen career and/or educational pursuit. Help me to use my talents for Your glory and the benefit of who you have called me to serve and uplift.

Wherever you plant me, give me the ability to make a positive impact and influence in my workplace, reflecting Your love, integrity, and values in all that I do. Help me to maintain faith and trust in Your timing and provision as I navigate the places you have appointed me to serve and grow.

Thank you for the peace of knowing that You have a perfect plan for my life. So as I trust your plan, give me balance and strategy to execute and excel. God, help me to have the wisdom to balance work responsibilities with my personal life. Prioritizing time for You, my family, and myself. Guide me in building meaningful relationships and networking connections that support my career growth and help me fulfill Your purpose. I pray that whatever I do becomes a means of glorifying You and serving others in accordance with Your will. Today, I place all these things in Your hands, trusting that You will lead me on paths that fulfill Your purpose for my life. In Jesus' name, amen,

DAY 18: A PRAYER FOR PURPOSE.

On day eighteen of this spiritual journey, I would like to help you develop a prayer for purpose. When we seek understanding for purpose, we must understand the priority of our lives. We have to come to a conclusion about whose priority matters. When you pursue purpose, you must be willing to establish up front if you're willing to walk His way when His way feels uncomfortable. But when His will is your priority, you've made an intentional decision to walk in His purpose over your preference. Therefore, we should concentrate our prayer on achieving clarity in understanding our purpose. Strength and courage to execute it. Alignment with God's will and opportunities to grow in your spiritual relationship with Him. Pray for the discipline to be faithful and obedient, even in seasons of challenge and discomfort. Ask to monitor and manage your impact and influence. Seek perseverance and service with gratitude and humility.

When we seek God for prayers for purpose, we find ourselves praying more purposeful prayers. Maybe as you bring this 21-day journey closer to an end, it's time to consider your own prayer targets and areas that you want to develop prayers in. While this book is designed to get you started, ultimately this is your moment to learn to feel more comfortable building your personal prayer life. So today, pray that God would expand your spirit and take you deeper in purpose! Are you ready? Let's pray...

God, today I am asking that you would give me the clarity and understanding of the purpose you have for my life. I ask that you would give me the wisdom and discernment to recognize the paths that you are placing me on. Help me to not fight against your direction in my life. Help me to identify when you are shifting me and things around me in order for your purpose to be fulfilled in me. God, today I ask that you would give me discernment to decipher your plan for my life with confidence, conviction, and clarity.

God I ask for strength and courage to embrace and fulfill the purpose you have designed for my life. Today, I choose to trust you, even if what I am facing is challenging. I ask that you would give me the strength to carry the weariness of waiting and help me to wait with good courage. God, help me follow your will as you work in my life. Help me to relinquish my desires to give room for your purpose to fulfill me, as I fulfill it. God, I ask that you would help me to follow your lead. As I trust the plans you have for my life are designed to bring me to an expected end. God, lead me to opportunities for spiritual growth and personal development that will equip me to fulfill my purpose and serve you effectively. God, give me the ability to be faithful and obedient to follow your leading and stay committed to the path you have set before me. Help me remain steadfast in pursuing your purpose for my life, even in the face of challenges and uncertainties.

God, Show me how my purpose can impact and bless others. So that I may be a source of light, hope, and encouragement to those around me. In all things, help me to approach our purpose with gratitude and humility, recognizing that it is ultimately your work in and through us. Thank you, Lord, for the privilege of understanding and fulfilling the purpose you have for me. In Jesus' name, amen.

DAY 19: A PRAYER FOR DIRECTION.

On day nineteen of this spiritual journey, I would like to help you develop a prayer for direction. When we seek God's direction through prayer, we can find solace, clarity, and a profound sense of purpose. When seeking guidance from God, it is essential to ask for wisdom, discernment, and a readiness to stick to His plan. Also, it may be advantageous to seek God's direction when making important decisions, trying to find clarity regarding our purpose. Finding strength to overcome challenges and finding peace during times of uncertainty.

Prayer has the power to guide us towards a life filled with meaning and satisfaction by aligning our desires and actions with purpose. When we pray for direction and give God the opportunity to speak back to us, we give His voice room to echo the blueprint of His will for us, regardless of where it leads us. So when we pray for direction today, we must pray that God releases a strategy that leads us to success in every area of our lives. We must pray that God's will is done, no matter how challenging the road to purpose may be. If we believe that God is causing it to work for us, we must trust

His direction for our lives in every season. Are you ready? Let's pray...

God, today I want to thank you for the blessing of communion with you! Without it, I wouldn't know which way to go. Without the ability to hear your voice, I'd be like a ship without a sail. So, God, today I pray that you show me direction. Today, my heart seeks to know the way that you want me to go. God, I know that life has pulled me in various directions. But today, I ask that you would center me on your compass for my life. Help me to rest, knowing that your path for me is greater than anything the world can provide for me. God, give me the strength to live a life of sacrifice to your will for me. Give me the clarity that I need to discern your direction.

I pray for open doors that direct me to the new levels you have for me! Help me to disconnect from anything that is not moving in the direction you have defined for me! Open doors of opportunity that are in line with your will, and close those that lead me astray. Help me recognize the signs and signals that you place before me as I navigate the choices and decisions that lie ahead.

My prayer is for forward! I pray for forward movement, forward thinking, forward living, and forward planning! God, help me to live in the expectation that you are a rewarder of those who diligently seek you. So God, I seek you because I know you are there to be found!

So thank you for never leaving me! Even when I wasn't walking in your direction! Thank you for staying by my side when I didn't understand what you wanted for me! Thank you for the grace and mercy you provide for me that allow me to move in a forward direction! Thank you for the grace to start fresh, start new, and start over. Thank you that what was is no more, and what's to come is only in your hands! So God, give me the strength to trust your way and your direction. In Jesus name, amen.

DAY 20: A PRAYER FOR PROTECTION.

On day twenty of this spiritual journey, I would like to help you develop a prayer for protection. When we pray for God's protection, we ask God to send ministering angels to our side to aid, guide, and keep us! Do you know that God has sent angel armies to guard and cover you in your coming and going? "For He will command His angels concerning you to keep you in all your ways. They will lift you up in their hands so that you will not strike your foot against the stone." -Psalm 91:11-12. You literally have angels in the outfield. Ok, the Disney kid in me has arisen. But, picture it: it's the bottom of the ninth in your life, and the bases are loaded. But here comes God with angels to make up for what you are missing, so that you can make it! That's what it means to have God's protection in your life. It's like a love story: when the girl goes to step into a puddle of mud and there's the guy madly in love with her, there to throw his jacket down, so that she never knew the impending disaster. That's how God's protection is in our lives. He covers us in such a way that we don't even know how bad the fall could have been. His protection keeps us from the residue of the trials and tests we face in every facet of life. Thank God for the blood. Today, as we pray, let us pray for protection, guidance, and shielding from God. knowing that He is there to protect us from all harm. Are you ready? Let's pray...

God, today I come before you, asking that you would place your protection over my life, my home, my family, everyone connected to me, and this nation. God, I ask that you would send your blood to fight for and cover my future in spite of the immaturity and traumas of my past. Today I am asking that you would watch over us, keep us, sustain us not just physically but also emotionally. God, I ask that you give us the strength and self-discipline we need to confront the challenges we face with a heart and humility, knowing you are fighting for us. So today, because we know You as a great champion, I believe you to be my great defender, my shield, and my buckler. Thank you. You are my rock and my sword. God, today I thank you for your power that constantly wars against spiritual wickedness in high places on my behalf.

God, I ask that you would cause your protection to overshadow my home and everyone connected to me from dangers seen and unseen. Surround me with your love and care, and help me to grow in your peace as you cover everything concerning me. God, today I ask that you would give me the wisdom I need to trust you for my future and follow the plan you set for me. So protect me, even if the enemy you hide is me!

Protect me from enemies and "inner me's.". Protect me from the voices with-in and the voices with-out. God protect me from opinions that are designed to distract me and discourage me and from every voice that causes me to doubt. God, I pray for protection. Protect our cities, our streets, our at-risk youth, and our minorities. Protect marginalized people and those whose rights have been violated by others, God. I pray today that you help me to make decisions that are reflective of your desire being priority in my life! So keep me and I'll be kept. In Jesus' name. Amen

DAY 21: A PRAYER FOR SYSTEMS. OF THIS WORLD.

On day twenty of this spiritual journey, I would like to help you develop a prayer for the systems of this world. On day twenty-one of this spiritual journey, I would like to help you develop a prayer for the systems of the world. When praying for the systems of the world, such as the economy, government, and justice systems, we must consider that often, those who are most impacted by these systems are those who have once been victims of them. If you have never struggled through poverty, injustice, and messy politics, then perhaps you don't understand the importance of praying for the systems of this world. But daily, we must raise a standard and pray for everything from Capitol Hill to the White House to every local decision-making authority in this country.

These systems have impacted and marginalized people. These systems consistently "other" people who aren't part of the stereotype of American "standard." These systems have frequently left our world in a state of extreme imbalance. So when we pray, we must pray that God uproots corruption, malice, and hidden agendas. That God would shine His light on injustices and bring righteous indignation to those who have been unfairly treated. We must pray for lawmakers and decision-makers, as what they do affects our world. At the time of this writing, we are still standing by idly as a country, watching a genocide in Gaza.

When we pray, we ask God to vindicate those affected by these systems, and we ask God to uphold and regulate them. We pray for just and fair governance, economic stability, moral integrity, social justice, environmental stewardship, and fair politics. Are you ready? Let's pray...

God, today I want to thank you for the blessing of this 21-day spiritual journey. Thank you for the lessons I've learned, the discipline I've gained, and the devotion we've shared. Today, I am asking that your presence and power would rest with me! Today, I ask that you touch and take control of the systems of this world. God, while we are not conformed to this world, we operate by its economy, its government, and its justice systems. But God, today I ask for equality and fairness to rule our world.

God, I pray that you would help those who are handling the heaviness of social and political injustices. God, please help guide our leaders and decision-makers. I pray that you will give them the discernment to govern justly and compassionately. I pray that you will raise up leaders who carry your heart and your passion, even in the area of influencing policies and practices.

God, give us the courage to speak up against injustice and stand up for the oppressed and the marginalized. Today I pray for the spirits of those who have been "othered" in life. I pray that you would cause them to see the beauty of your unique creation in their lives. God, I thank you that our government sits on your shoulders! Thank you! That the heart of the king is in your hand, and you turn it whatever way you will. So, spirit of the living God, take control and maintain your control. Cover us from lack, want, and need right now.

God bless this nation, this country, our political systems, and our justice system. God help this economy, increase this job market, and create new wealth and opportunities within our country. I pray for new business owners and wealth builders to arise! God, touch those who are seated in positions of power and authority; touch those who influence children and policies. Our next generation's leaders and those who enforce our laws are under your care. God, today we ask for you to get all into the systems of this world and take control, and we believe you for a new thing in Jesus name, amen!

CONCLUDING MESSGE

Welp, we did it! 21 days of walking through some areas that govern our lives spiritually and naturally. We walked through 21 days of empowering our spirits in order to take authority over those areas. This is where you must do the work! It's your turn to go through the next 2 days developing your own prayer targets! Every season may bring new areas of focus for our prayers. Maybe this is your moment to let God direct your life in a new way! Maybe you're saying, I like these 21 areas! Perfect, let's do it again! This time, grab a journal and let's hear your morning cup! Let's hear your language of focus and meditation with God. I am always here cheering you on as you daily surrender your heart to God in prayer!

As you sip from the Morning Cup of prayer each day for 21 days, may your soul be nourished, your spirit refreshed, and your heart strengthened. Let this devotional guide you to start your day in communion with God, seeking wisdom, grace, and peace. May each prayer be a reminder of the unending love and faithfulness of our God, leading you on a journey of deeper connection and spiritual growth. Embrace the stillness of the morning and let your prayers light the path before you, filling each day with the light of hope and purpose.

Oh, and "If you agree with this prayer, send it to someone that you know and believe that the same power that's at work for you right now is transcending your location and meeting them at the point of their need. In Jesus name."

That means pass this book on, like you share those prayers! :) I'm out! -M

ABOUT THE AUTHOR

Rev. Marissa R. Farrow, a native of Baltimore, MD, was born on June 19, 1989, to Bishop Robert E. Farrow and Evangelist Jacqueline Farrow, pastors of Mt. Calvary Church & Ministries, where she was launched into ministry. On March 4, 2007, Marissa began her public ministry, preaching her initial sermon entitled “The Unshakable Call."

After a few years of trying to “find the right pace,” she began her academic journey and currently holds a Bachelor of Science degree in Business Administration from Livingstone College in Salisbury, NC. And a Masters of Divinity Degree from the Samuel Dewitt Proctor School of Theology at Virginia Union University. She is also a proud spring 2015 initiate of Alpha Kappa Alpha Sorority, Inc.

Since her ordination in 2013, Elder Farrow has served under the tutelage of the Rev. Drs. Floyd and Elaine Flake at the Greater Allen A.M.E. Cathedral of New York as a preaching assistant, special outreach project coordinator, and social media director.

Having been blessed by God with exponential doors of opportunity, she considers herself blessed to preach the gospel of Jesus Christ all across the world, much of it before the age of 30. Bringing her to share for events such as the International Pastors and Leaders Conference, the International AIM Convention for the Church of God in Christ Inc., Guest Speaker at the final 3 Woman Thou Art Loosed Conferences for Bishop T.D. Jakes, and one of the youngest morning preachers for the distinguished 110th Hampton University ministers conference.

She has also had the privilege of sharing the gospel in Nigeria, Lagos, West Africa, Dubai, and London, England. She has also made numerous appearances on the Word Network.

She is the author of two books: Delivered From Dysfunction: A 7-Step Guide to a Better You and The Amazing Weight. She anticipates the release of "The Morning Cup," a 21-day prayer devotional that draws inspiration from her growing #ViralPrayerCommunity on Instagram, reaching over 1.1 million views monthly. She is also the owner of Brown By Marissa, a Christ-centered fashion brand.

She is a praiser, prayer warrior, preacher, podcast host, producer, and the proud “BFF” of her “God Gift," Shamol-Ali and, She is just getting started.

BOOK CITATIONS & REFRENCES

"Jeremiah 29:12-13 (AMP)." n.d. Bible Gateway. https://www.biblegateway.com/passage/?search=Jeremiah%2029%3A12-13&version=AMP.

"Lamentations 3:21-24 (NIV)." n.d. Bible Gateway. https://www.biblegateway.com/passage/?search=Lamentations%203%3A21-24&version=NIV.

"Lamentations 3:22-23 (AMP)." n.d. Bible Gateway. https://www.biblegateway.com/passage/?search=Lamentations%203%3A22-23&version=AMP.

"Mark 1 (NIV)." n.d. Bible Gateway. https://www.biblegateway.com/passage/?search=Mark%201&version=NIV.

"Matthew 17:19-21 (AMP)." n.d. Bible Gateway. https://www.biblegateway.com/passage/?search=Matthew%2017:19-21&version=AMP.

"John 15:26 (AMP)." n.d. Bible Gateway. https://www.biblegateway.com/passage/?search=John%2015%3A26&version=AMP.

Made in the USA
Columbia, SC
08 July 2024

9e5918d6-813f-46bc-92d9-d0620b5fc248R01